S0-BXW-000

Sugar and Spice

Cookbook for girls

hinkler

Published by Hinkler Books Pty Ltd
45–55 Fairchild Street
Heatherton Victoria 3202 Australia
www.hinkler.com.au

hinkler

Design and layout © Hinkler Books Pty Ltd 2012
Food photography and recipe development © StockFood, The Food Media Agency

Design: Julie Thompson and Hinkler Design Studio
Typesetting: MPS Limited
Prepress: Graphic Print Group

Images © Shutterstock.com: Flower cupcakes © Ruth Black (cover);
Heart pattern © LiveStock; Seamless hearts © Irmairma; Cupcake icon © gst.

All rights reserved. No part of this publication may be reproduced, stored in a
retrieval system, or transmitted in any way or by any means, electronic, mechanical,
photocopying, recording or otherwise, without the prior written permission of Hinkler
Books Pty Ltd.

ISBN: 978 1 7430 8638 4

Printed and bound in China

Contents

Introduction	4
Main Meals	6
Desserts	26
Baked Goods	46
Party Food	66
Sleepover Treats	86
Picnic Lunch	106
Weights and Measures	126
Index	128

Let's Get Cooking!

Learning to cook can be easy and fun, and a great skill to have when you're growing up. Best of all, you can make delicious meals and mouth-watering treats to share with your family and friends.

Take some time to look through the recipes and see which ones you want to cook first. It doesn't matter whether you choose a recipe from the beginning, middle or end of the book: each recipe is explained in simple terms so you can start cooking straight away.

Symbols

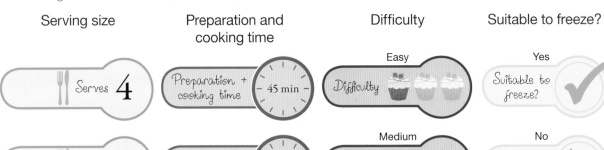

| Serving size | Preparation and cooking time | Difficulty | Suitable to freeze? |

Serves 4

Preparation + cooking time — 45 min

Easy — Difficulty

Yes — Suitable to freeze?

Makes 10

Preparation + chilling time — 12 hr 20 min

Medium — Difficulty

No — Suitable to freeze?

Expert! — Difficulty

Nutrition

It's good to know what you're eating, so each recipe includes a nutrition panel that looks like this:

Each breakdown is per serving (for example, per cupcake or per drumstick) unless it says otherwise.

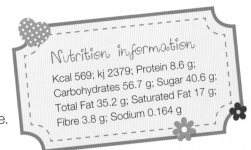

Nutrition information
Kcal 569; kj 2379; Protein 8.6 g; Carbohydrates 56.7 g; Sugar 40.6 g; Total Fat 35.2 g; Saturated Fat 17 g; Fibre 3.8 g; Sodium 0.164 g

Handy Hints

You can experiment with each recipe to find out what works best for your tastebuds!

Look at the flowers for extra ingredient ideas.

Follow the handy cooking tips in the hearts.

Weights and Measurements

This book makes things easy by using metric measurements (g, kg, mL, L), imperial measurements (oz, lb, fl oz) and also cups and spoons. Remember:

* Use the same-sized cup each time
* Learn your spoon sizes: teaspoon (tsp) and tablespoon (tbsp) are the most commonly used in this book
* Use a measuring jug for liquids
* Weights and measures charts are included on pages 126 and 127

Clean Cooking

Make sure your cooking area is clean before you start, and ALWAYS leave it clean and tidy when you have finished. That includes doing the washing up!

* Wash your hands before you start to cook
* Wear an apron to protect your clothes
* Use separate utensils and chopping boards for raw meat

Stay Safe

Before you start to cook, read through the recipe instructions. Gather together all your equipment and ingredients. Then look for this icon next to the steps:
This means that you might need to ask an adult for help for that step.

* Always ask an adult for permission before you start cooking
* Use a dry oven mitt or oven gloves to move items in and out of the oven
* Hot items can burn; be very careful near boiling liquids, when lifting off a lid or when using the stove
* Pay attention when using knives or scissors, and ask an adult for help if you need it

Tomato Soup with Croutons

Ingredients:

For the soup:
2 tbsp olive oil
1 shallot, diced
1 large carrot, diced
1 tsp plain (all-purpose) flour
400 g | 14 oz canned chopped
    tomatoes
600 mL | 21 fl oz | 2½ cups
    vegetable stock (broth)
salt
1–2 pinches white (granulated) sugar

For the croutons:
2 slices white bread, cut into cubes
2–3 tbsp grated cheese
    (e.g. cheddar, gouda)

To garnish:
parsley

Method:

1 Heat 1 tablespoon oil in a large pan and gently cook the diced shallot and carrot until tender.

2 Add the flour and cook for 1 minute. Add the tomatoes and stock (broth), cover and simmer for 20 minutes. Allow to cool slightly, then puree in a food processor or blender until smooth. Return to the pan and season with salt and sugar to taste.

3 For the croutons: heat the oven to 180°C (160° fan/350°F/gas 4). Grease a baking tray (sheet).

4 Put the bread cubes on the baking tray and drizzle with the remaining oil. Bake for about 8 minutes until just golden. Sprinkle with the cheese and bake for a further 2–3 minutes until the cheese has melted.

5 Reheat the soup and ladle into bowls. Serve scattered with croutons and garnish with parsley.

Nutrition information
Kcal 151; kj 631; Protein 4.5 g;
Carbohydrates 14.5 g; Sugar 7.6 g;
Total Fat 8.8 g; Saturated Fat 2.5 g;
Fibre 3 g; Sodium 0.332 g

This soup can be made up to 2 days before and kept in the refrigerator.

Spaghetti Bolognaise

Ingredients:

4 tbsp olive oil
1 onion, diced
100 g | 3½ oz bacon, diced
2 cloves garlic
1 tsp chopped oregano
450 g | 16 oz minced (ground) beef
400 g | 14 oz canned
   chopped tomatoes
330 mL | 12 fl oz | 1⅓ cup beef stock
   (broth)
1 tbsp balsamic vinegar
1 pinch white (granulated) sugar
450 g | 16 oz spaghetti
freshly ground black pepper
4 tbsp grated Parmesan cheese

Method:

1 Heat half the olive oil in a large pan. Add the onion and bacon and cook gently without browning for 5 minutes, stirring.

2 Stir in the garlic and oregano and continue cooking for 1 minute. Add the beef and cook until browned.

3 Add the tomatoes and their juice, the stock (broth), vinegar and sugar. Bring to a simmer and cook for about 20 minutes, until most of the liquid has evaporated.

4 Bring a large pan of lightly salted water to the boil, and cook the spaghetti according to the instructions on the packet, until tender.

5 Drain the spaghetti well and return to the pan. Drizzle with the remaining olive oil and season with freshly ground black pepper.

6 Divide the spaghetti between 4 warmed serving plates and top with the sauce. Sprinkle with the cheese.

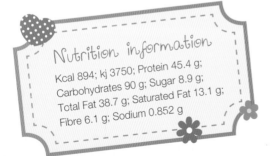

Nutrition information

Kcal 894; kj 3750; Protein 45.4 g;
Carbohydrates 90 g; Sugar 8.9 g;
Total Fat 38.7 g; Saturated Fat 13.1 g;
Fibre 6.1 g; Sodium 0.852 g

For a spicier version add a dash of Tabasco (hot) sauce with the tomatoes.

Quesadillas

Ingredients:

3 tbsp olive oil
1 clove garlic, chopped
200 g | 7 oz chorizo cooking
    sausage, sliced
350 g | 12 oz boiled potatoes, sliced
6 spring onions (scallions), cut in half
salt and black pepper
4 large flour tortillas
200 g | 7 oz | 2 cups grated cheese
4–6 lettuce leaves

Method:

1 Heat 2 tablespoons olive oil in a large frying pan (skillet) and fry the garlic, chorizo and potatoes for about 5 minutes until lightly browned.

2 Add the spring onions (scallions) and cook for 1 minute. Season to taste with salt and pepper.

3 Divide the mixture between the tortillas and sprinkle with the cheese. Add the lettuce leaves and fold over the tortillas to make a half moon shape.

4 Brush the tortillas with a little of the remaining oil.

5 Heat a dry frying pan and cook the tortillas until the cheese has melted. Serve immediately.

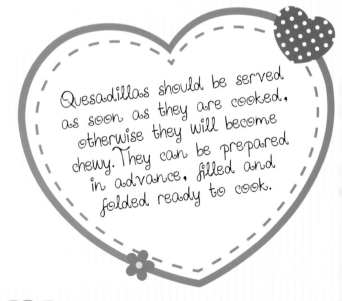

Quesadillas should be served as soon as they are cooked, otherwise they will become chewy. They can be prepared in advance, filled and folded ready to cook.

Nutrition information

Kcal 755; kj 3162; Protein 30.9 g;
Carbohydrates 76.8 g; Sugar 3.8 g;
Total Fat 38.1 g; Saturated Fat 17 g;
Fibre 5 g; Sodium 0.913 g

Beef Skewers with Peanut Sauce

Ingredients:

450 g | 16 oz sirloin or
    fillet steak, cubed

For the marinade:
6 tbsp soy sauce
6 tbsp teriyaki sauce
1 clove garlic, crushed
1 tsp coriander (cilantro) seeds,
    crushed

For the peanut sauce:
225 g | 8 oz crunchy peanut butter
3 cloves garlic, crushed
50 mL | 1¾ fl oz | 10 tsp soy sauce
2 tbsp lime juice
½ tsp chilli flakes
120 mL | 4 fl oz | ½ cup coconut milk
oil for brushing

Method:

1 Push the cubed meat onto soaked wooden skewers.

2 Mix together all the marinade ingredients. Place the beef skewers in a shallow dish and pour over the marinade. Cover the dish and leave to marinate for at least 4 hours.

3 For the sauce: put the peanut butter and garlic into a food processor or blender.

4 Mix together the soy sauce, lime juice, chilli flakes and coconut milk. With the motor running, pour the mixture slowly into the blender until the sauce is thick. If the sauce is too thick, add 1–2 tablespoons water. Put into a serving bowl.

5 Heat the grill (broiler).

6 Brush the marinated beef with oil and grill (broil) for 6–8 minutes, turning halfway through, until cooked through.

7 Serve with the peanut sauce for dipping.

Nutrition information
Kcal 693; kj 2870; Protein 32.2 g;
Carbohydrates 10.6 g; Sugar 6.4 g;
Total Fat 57.9 g; Saturated Fat 18.5 g;
Fibre 0.2 g; Sodium 1.353 g

Soak wooden skewers in cold water for 30 minutes before using, to avoid burning.

Main Meals

Bean and Rice Burritos

Ingredients:

125 mL | 4½ fl oz | ½ cup passata (tomatoes, puréed then sieved to remove skin)
40 mL | 1½ fl oz | 8 tsp water
1 pinch chilli powder
½ tsp ground cumin
½ tsp onion salt
¼ tsp paprika
1 pinch cayenne pepper
1 pinch white (granulated) sugar
½ tbsp vinegar
200 g | 7 oz long-grain rice
420 g | 15 oz canned red kidney beans, drained
6 flour tortillas
170 g | 6 oz | 1½ cups grated cheddar cheese

Method:

1 Put the passata, water, spices, sugar and vinegar in a pan and bring to a boil over a low heat, stirring. Reduce the heat and simmer for 10–15 minutes until smooth and thickened. Remove from the heat and set aside.

2 Cook the rice in boiling salted water according to the packet instructions until tender. Drain the rice and stir in the beans and sauce. Heat gently, mixing well, until piping hot.

3 Heat a frying pan (skillet) and warm the tortillas on each side.

4 Divide the bean mixture between the tortillas and sprinkle with the cheese. Fold sides and ends over the filling and roll up.

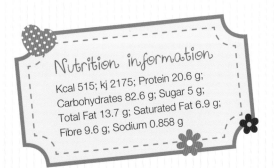

Nutrition information

Kcal 515; kj 2175; Protein 20.6 g; Carbohydrates 82.6 g; Sugar 5 g; Total Fat 13.7 g; Saturated Fat 6.9 g; Fibre 9.6 g; Sodium 0.858 g

To reheat the burritos: wrap in foil and place in a warm oven for a few minutes until heated through.

Try black beans instead of red kidney beans.

You can use brown rice instead of white rice.

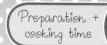

Pasta and Vegetable Bake

Ingredients:

500 g | 18 oz spaghetti
salt
2 sticks celery, cut into thin strips
200 mL | 7 fl oz | ⅞ cup cream, 48% fat
100 mL | 3½ fl oz | 7 tbsp milk
2 eggs
2 tbsp creme fraiche
2 tbsp grated Parmesan cheese
freshly ground pepper

To garnish:
chives

Method:

1 Heat the oven to 200°C (180° fan/400°F/gas 6). Grease 4 ramekins or ovenproof glass dishes.

2 Cook the spaghetti in boiling salted water until just tender. Drain and set aside.

3 Cook the celery strips in boiling salted water for 3–4 minutes, then drain well.

4 Divide the spaghetti and celery between the ramekins.

5 Beat together the cream, milk, eggs and creme fraiche until smooth. Stir in the cheese and season to taste with salt and pepper. Pour over the spaghetti and celery.

6 Bake for about 25 minutes until golden and bubbling. Serve garnished with chives.

Nutrition information
Kcal 679; kj 2863; Protein 24.3 g;
Carbohydrates 95.4 g; Sugar 6.9 g;
Total Fat 24.9 g; Saturated Fat 13.4 g;
Fibre 5.1 g; Sodium 0.521 g

Try leeks instead of celery.

Main Meals

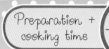

Chicken and Vegetable Skewers with Rice

Ingredients:

2 tbsp olive oil
1 tbsp vinegar
1 clove garlic, crushed
½ tsp salt
¼ tsp freshly ground black pepper
1 large zucchini (courgette), sliced
4 cherry tomatoes
4 button mushrooms
450 g | 16 oz skinless boneless chicken
    breasts, cut into 2.5 cm (1 in) cubes

To serve:
boiled rice
lemon wedges
Greek yoghurt
oregano

Method:

1 Heat the grill (broiler) and lightly oil the grill rack.

2 Whisk together the olive oil, vinegar, garlic, salt and pepper. Add the vegetables and chicken and toss until well coated.

3 Thread alternating pieces of chicken, zucchini (courgettes), mushrooms and tomatoes on soaked wooden skewers.

4 Place the skewers on the grill rack and grill (broil) about 15 cm (6 in) from the heat for 5–7 minutes. Turn over the skewers and cook for a further 5 minutes, until the chicken is cooked through.

5 Arrange on a serving plate and serve with boiled rice, lemon wedges and a small bowl of Greek yoghurt garnished with oregano.

Nutrition information

Kcal 181; kj 758; Protein 28.1 g;
Carbohydrates 1.2 g; Sugar 1 g;
Total Fat 7 g; Saturated Fat 1.2 g;
Fibre 0.8 g; Sodium 0.560 g

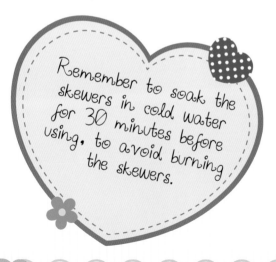

Remember to soak the skewers in cold water for 30 minutes before using, to avoid burning the skewers.

Main Meals

Macaroni and Cheese

Ingredients:

225 g | 8 oz | 2 cups grated sharp cheese, e.g. mature cheddar
50 g | 1¾ oz | ½ cup grated Parmesan cheese
50 g | 1¾ oz | 1 cup fresh breadcrumbs
1 pinch salt
300 g | 11 oz | 3 cups macaroni
700 mL | 25 fl oz | 3 cups milk
50 g | 1¾ oz | ¼ cup butter
50 g | 1¾ oz | ½ cup plain (all-purpose) flour
1 tsp Dijon mustard

Method:

1 Heat the oven to 190°C (170° fan/375°F/gas 5). Butter a baking dish, about 30 x 20 x 5.5 cm (12 x 8 x 2 in).

2 Mix 25 g (1 oz) of the cheese and ⅓ of the Parmesan with the breadcrumbs. Set aside.

3 Mix the remaining cheeses together and set aside.

4 Bring a large pan of water to a boil. Add the salt and macaroni, stir and return to a boil. Simmer for 8 minutes, or cook according to the packet instructions, until almost but not quite cooked through – stirring occasionally to prevent sticking.

5 Warm the milk. Melt the butter separately in a large pan and stir in the flour. Cook for 1 minute, stirring, then remove from the heat.

6 Pour ⅓ of the warm milk into the flour mixture and beat well until smooth. Add another ⅓ of the milk and continue beating well until smooth. Pour in the final ⅓ of milk and beat until smooth.

7 Heat the sauce, stirring, until thickened and smooth. Reduce the heat and simmer for 4 minutes until shiny. Remove from the heat and stir in the cheese and mustard. If the sauce is too thick add a little more milk.

8 Drain the macaroni in a colander and gently stir into the sauce to coat completely.

9 Tip the macaroni and cheese into the baking dish and scatter the cheese breadcrumbs on top. Bake for 12–15 minutes until beginning to bubble around the edges.

10 Heat the grill (broiler). Grill (broil) for 5 minutes to brown the crumbs. Serve immediately.

Nutrition information

Kcal 824; kj 3452; Protein 35.9 g; Carbohydrates 80.5 g; Sugar 10.4 g; Total Fat 41.9 g; Saturated Fat 25.8 g; Fibre 3.9 g; Sodium 0.703 g

Make sure your macaroni is a little undercooked, as when it goes into the oven, the macaroni will continue to cook. If you cook it completely beforehand, it will become overcooked.

Main Meals

Serves 6 | Preparation + cooking time 1 hr 40 min | Difficulty | Suitable to freeze? X

Pizza with Ham, Corn and Mushrooms

Ingredients:

For the base:

300 g | 11 oz | 2¾ cups strong bread flour
1 tsp instant yeast
1 tsp salt
200 mL | 7 fl oz | ⅞ cup warm water
1 tbsp olive oil, plus extra for drizzling

For the topping:

200 g | 7 oz | 2 cups grated cheddar cheese
250 g | 9 oz tomatoes, diced
salt
freshly ground black pepper
150 g | 5 oz cooked ham, sliced
100 g | 3½ oz mushrooms, sliced
198 g | 7 oz canned kernel corn (corn kernels or sweetcorn), drained

Method:

1 For the base: mix together the flour, yeast and salt in a mixing bowl. Make a well in the centre and pour in the water and oil. Mix to a soft, fairly wet dough.

2 Turn onto a lightly floured surface and knead for 5 minutes until smooth. Put into a lightly greased bowl, cover with a tea towel and leave to rise until doubled in size – about 1 hour.

3 Heat the oven to 200°C (180° fan/400°F/gas 6). Line a baking tray (sheet) with non-stick baking paper.

4 Quickly knead the dough and roll out into a large round about 25 cm (10 in) in diameter. Place on the baking tray.

5 For the topping: brush the dough with olive oil and sprinkle with some of the cheese. Place the tomatoes on top and season with salt and pepper. Add the remaining cheese, ham, mushrooms and corn.

6 Drizzle with oil and bake for about 20 minutes until the base is cooked, the cheese is bubbling and the tomatoes and mushrooms are tender.

Nutrition information

Kcal 497; kj 2077; Protein 20.7 g; Carbohydrates 40 g; Sugar 2.8 g; Total Fat 29.3 g; Saturated Fat 9.9 g; Fibre 3.5 g; Sodium 1.397 g

Add a sprinkling of chopped fresh herbs (oregano, basil, etc.) as soon as the pizza comes out of the oven.

For a change, spread the uncooked pizza base with 2-3 tablespoons of pesto before adding the topping.

23

Main Meals

Fish Finger Dinner

Ingredients:

50 g | 1¾ oz | 1 cup white
    breadcrumbs
1 lemon, finely grated zest
2 tbsp chopped dill (dill weed)
2 tbsp chopped parsley
1 pinch salt
500 g | 18 oz skinless white fish fillets,
    cut into 3 x 10 cm (1 x 4 in) pieces
2 tbsp plain (all-purpose) flour
salt and pepper
1 egg, beaten
oil for frying

Method:

1 Mix together the breadcrumbs, lemon zest, herbs and salt.

2 Dust each fish piece with the flour and season with a little salt and pepper. Shake off any excess, then dip into the egg, then the breadcrumbs.

3 Heat the oil to a depth of about 1 cm (½ in) in a large frying pan (skillet). Fry the fish fingers a few at a time for 1–2 minutes on each side, until crisp and golden and the fish is cooked.

4 Drain on absorbent kitchen paper, and keep warm while you cook the rest.

5 Serve with potato wedges (see page 78) and mushy peas.

Nutrition information
Kcal 211; kj 886; Protein 26.7 g;
Carbohydrates 13.8 g; Sugar 0.8 g;
Total Fat 5.7 g; Saturated Fat 0.9 g;
Fibre 1.4 g; Sodium 0.154 g

Replace half the breadcrumbs with polenta (cornmeal) for a crunchier version.

Try sesame seeds instead of the herbs.

Main Meals

Summer Berry Pudding

Ingredients:

225 g | 8 oz | 1½ cups raspberries
225 g | 8 oz | 1 cup strawberries
100 g | 3½ oz | 1 cup redcurrants
225 g | 8 oz | 2 cups blueberries
225 g | 8 oz | 1½ cups blackberries
80 g | 3 oz | ⅓ cup caster
    (berry) sugar
3 tbsp water
5–6 slices thick white bread,
    crusts removed

To decorate:
200 g | 7 oz | 1½ cups whole berries

Method:

1 Gently heat the fruit, sugar and water in a pan until the sugar dissolves and the fruit juices start to run. Simmer for 2–3 minutes and set aside.

2 Use 2–3 slices of bread to line the base and sides of a 900 g (2 lb) loaf tin, cutting to fit and overlapping if necessary.

3 Spoon in the warm fruit and juices and cover with the remaining bread. Cover with cling film and place the tin on a plate to catch any drips. Place a saucer on top of the tin and weight down (scale weights or cans of food are ideal). Chill overnight.

4 Remove the weights and cling film. Turn out the pudding carefully and scatter the berries on top. Cut into slices to serve.

Nutrition information
Kcal 232; kj 987; Protein 6.4 g;
Carbohydrates 52 g; Sugar 27.2 g;
Total Fat 1.3 g; Saturated Fat 0.3 g;
Fibre 7 g; Sodium 0.266 g

For a special treat, use brioche or fruit bread instead of plain white bread.

Chocolate Fondue

Ingredients:

350 g | 12 oz plain (dark) chocolate,
   60% cocoa solids
150 mL | 5 fl oz | ⅔ cup cream,
   48% fat
75 g | 2½ oz | ⅓ cup dark brown sugar
1 tsp vanilla extract

To serve:
bananas, cut into chunks
strawberries, halved
marshmallows

Method:

1 Put all the ingredients into a pan and heat very gently until the chocolate and sugar have melted. Stir gently until smooth.

2 Pour into a chocolate fondue pot and keep warm over the burner. Serve with the bananas, strawberries and marshmallows speared on fondue forks.

Serve with chunks of melon, orange segments, cherries or cubes of sponge cake.

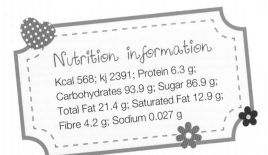

Nutrition information

Kcal 568; kj 2391; Protein 6.3 g;
Carbohydrates 93.9 g; Sugar 86.9 g;
Total Fat 21.4 g; Saturated Fat 12.9 g;
Fibre 4.2 g; Sodium 0.027 g

For a choc-orange taste, swap the vanilla extract for 2 tbsp of orange juice.

Desserts

Raspberry Meringues

Ingredients:

5 egg whites
300 g | 11 oz | 1½ cups caster (berry) sugar
4 tbsp chopped almonds

To decorate:
300 mL | 11 fl oz | 1⅓ cups cream, 48% fat
200 g | 7 oz | 1½ cups raspberries
3 tbsp chopped toasted almonds
1 lime, grated zest

To serve:
lime wedges
raspberries

Method:

1 For the meringues: set the oven to its lowest setting. Line a large baking tray (sheet) with non-stick baking paper.

2 Whisk the egg whites with an electric whisk until foamy. Gradually whisk in the sugar, whisking constantly until the mixture is stiff and glossy. Gently fold in the almonds.

3 Spoon 10–12 rounds onto the baking tray and bake for 3–5 hours (depending on your oven and the size of the meringues) until crisp on the outside, and sounding hollow when tapped on the base. Turn the oven off and leave the meringues in the oven until cold.

4 To decorate: whisk the cream until thick. Spoon a little cream onto the bases of half the meringues and top with a few raspberries and a sprinkle of almonds.

5 Gently place another meringue on top and spoon on a little cream and more raspberries and almonds. Sprinkle with lime zest and serve immediately with lime wedges and raspberries.

Nutrition information
Kcal 568; kj 2372; Protein 6.8 g;
Carbohydrates 56.1 g; Sugar 55.6 g;
Total Fat 36.7 g; Saturated Fat 17.5 g;
Fibre 1.1 g; Sodium 0.056 g

Egg whites at room temperature whisk better than chilled egg whites from the refrigerator.

It's important to add the sugar to the egg whites slowly, as it helps prevent the meringue from 'weeping' later.

Desserts

Strawberry and Chocolate Ice-Cream Sandwiches

Ingredients:

250 g | 9 oz | 2 cups
chopped strawberries
lemon juice
300 mL | 11 fl oz | 1⅓ cups cream,
48% fat
400 g | 14 oz canned condensed milk
pink food colouring (optional)
30 chocolate cookies

Method:

1 Puree the strawberries in a food processor or blender, then rub through a sieve into a bowl. Squeeze in a few drops of lemon juice.

2 Whisk the cream and condensed milk in a mixing bowl with an electric whisk until thick.

3 Fold in the strawberry puree and colouring if using. Spoon into a freezerproof container, cover and freeze for at least 4 hours.

4 Sandwich the cookies in pairs with the ice-cream and serve immediately or return to the freezer until ready to serve.

Add 2 teaspoons rosewater to the strawberry puree. Yum!

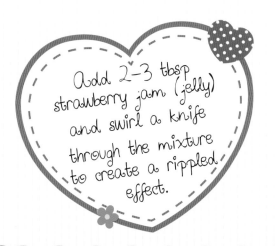

Add 2–3 tbsp strawberry jam (jelly) and swirl a knife through the mixture to create a rippled effect.

Nutrition information

Kcal 292; kj 1220; Protein 4.2 g;
Carbohydrates 29.5 g; Sugar 25.2 g;
Total Fat 18.3 g; Saturated Fat 11 g;
Fibre 0.2 g; Sodium 0.089 g

Desserts

Layered Cake with Raspberries and Cream

Ingredients:

450 g | 16 oz | 3 cups raspberries
400 mL | 14 fl oz | 1⅔ cups cream,
    48% fat
6 slices chocolate cake

Method:

1 Mash half the raspberries and divide between 6 serving glasses.

2 Whisk the cream until thick but not stiff and spoon a layer on top of the raspberries.

3 Crumble the cake roughly and divide between the glasses.

4 Top with a few whole raspberries and more cream. Top each with a raspberry and chill before serving.

You can use strawberries instead of raspberries.

Try plain cake or gingerbread instead of chocolate cake.

Nutrition information

Kcal 697; kj 2895; Protein 7.6 g;
Carbohydrates 42.5 g; Sugar 26.2 g;
Total Fat 56.4 g; Saturated Fat 27.1 g;
Fibre 4.2 g; Sodium 0.315 g

Desserts

Chocolate Mousse with Raspberry Sauce

Ingredients:

For the mousse:

200 g | 7 oz milk chocolate, 30% cocoa solids

400 mL | 14 fl oz | 1⅔ cups cream, 48% fat

55 g | 2 oz | ¼ cup white (granulated) sugar

1 tsp vanilla extract

For the sauce:

125 g | 4½ oz | 1 cup raspberries

1–2 tbsp icing (confectioner's) sugar

1 tbsp lemon juice

Method:

1 For the mousse: melt the chocolate in a heat-proof bowl over a pan of simmering (not boiling) water. Remove from the heat. Allow to cool.

2 Whisk the cream with the sugar and vanilla until thick but not stiff.

3 Gradually fold in the chocolate until combined. Spoon into serving glasses and chill for at least 4 hours until set.

4 For the sauce: put all the ingredients into a pan and slowly bring to a boil, stirring. Pour through a sieve into a serving bowl and leave to cool.

5 Spoon the sauce over the mousse to serve.

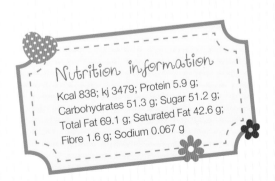

Nutrition information

Kcal 838; kj 3479; Protein 5.9 g; Carbohydrates 51.3 g; Sugar 51.2 g; Total Fat 69.1 g; Saturated Fat 42.6 g; Fibre 1.6 g; Sodium 0.067 g

Instead of milk chocolate, try a bar of flavoured chocolate, like orange or hazelnut.

You can add 1 teaspoon ground cinnamon and a pinch of grated nutmeg instead of the vanilla extract.

Grilled Fruit Skewers

Ingredients:

100 mL | 3½ fl oz | 7 tbsp orange juice
2 tsp cornflour (cornstarch)
1 tbsp honey
1 small pineapple, peeled and
 flesh cubed
1 mango, peeled and flesh cubed
8 strawberries, halved

Method:

1 Heat the grill (broiler).

2 Mix a little of the orange juice with the cornflour (cornstarch) and set aside. Heat the remaining orange juice and honey in a pan and whisk in the cornflour paste. Bring to a boil and cook for 1 minute. Remove from the heat and set aside.

3 Thread the fruits alternately onto soaked wooden skewers. Brush with the glaze and grill (broil) for 2 minutes.

4 Turn over and brush again with the glaze. Grill for a further 2–3 minutes until golden brown.

Soak the wooden skewers in cold water for 30 minutes before using, to avoid burning.

Nutrition information

Kcal 154; kj 654; Protein 1.2 g;
Carbohydrates 38.6 g; Sugar 27.5 g;
Total Fat 0.5 g; Saturated Fat 0.1 g;
Fibre 4.9 g; Sodium 0.03 g

Chocolate Whoopie Pies

Ingredients:

For the cakes:
110 g | 4 oz | ½ cup butter
110 g | 4 oz | ½ cup caster
    (berry) sugar
2 eggs
4 tbsp cocoa powder
225 g | 8 oz | 2 cups self-raising flour
½ tsp salt
1 tsp vanilla extract
120 mL | 4 fl oz | ½ cup milk

For the filling:
6 tbsp unsalted butter
100 g | 3½ oz | 1 cup icing
    (confectioner's) sugar
200 g | 7 oz marshmallow fluff (creme)
1 tsp vanilla extract

Method:

1 Heat the oven to 180°C (160° fan/350°F/gas 4). Line 3 large baking trays (sheets) with non-stick baking paper.

2 Beat the butter and sugar in a mixing bowl until light and fluffy. Gradually beat in the eggs until blended.

3 Sift in the cocoa, flour and salt and gently stir in until incorporated. Stir in the vanilla and milk.

4 Drop 2 tablespoons of the mixture at a time onto the baking trays, keeping them about 4 cm (2 in) apart.

5 Bake for about 15 minutes, until cooked through. Insert a skewer into the centre – it should come out clean. Cool on the baking trays for a few minutes, then place on a wire rack to cool completely.

6 For the filling: beat the butter until soft and creamy. Sift in the icing (confectioner's) sugar and beat until smooth. Beat in the marshmallow fluff (creme) and vanilla until well blended.

7 Turn half the cakes upside down and spread generously with the filling. Place the remaining cakes on top.

Nutrition information
Kcal 480; kj 2020; Protein 6.6 g;
Carbohydrates 70.9 g; Sugar 44.7 g;
Total Fat 20.9 g; Saturated Fat 12.5 g;
Fibre 2 g; Sodium 0.429 g

Use hazelnut, almond, orange or mint extract instead of vanilla for a different flavour.

Desserts

Raspberry Yoghurt Ice-Cream

Ingredients:

500 g | 18 oz | 4 cups raspberries
2 eggs, separated
125 g | 4½ oz | ½ cup white
   (granulated) sugar
2 tbsp lemon juice
500 mL | 18 fl oz | 2 cups cream,
   48% fat
200 mL | 7 fl oz | ⅞ cup
   raspberry yoghurt

Method:

1 Puree the raspberries in a food processor or blender, then push through a fine-mesh sieve into a bowl.

2 Whisk the egg yolks with the sugar until creamy. Stir in the lemon juice.

3 Whisk the cream and yoghurt until thick.

4 Whisk the egg whites until stiff. Fold the egg whites and the cream into the egg yolk mixture.

5 Gently stir about ⅕ of the cream mixture with ⅓ of the raspberry puree.

6 Mix the remaining cream mixture with the rest of the raspberry puree. Pour the lighter raspberry cream into 8 moulds or yoghurt cups. Freeze for 30 minutes.

7 Insert wooden sticks into the yoghurt cups and pour in the remaining raspberry cream. Freeze for 3–4 hours until completely frozen.

8 Shortly before serving, briefly dip the yoghurt cups into hot water, then carefully push the ice-cream out of the yoghurt cup onto a plate. Serve immediately.

Note: To make this ice-cream without eggs: puree the raspberries with 200 g (7 oz) yoghurt, the lemon juice and sugar to taste. Fold about 100 mL (3⅓ oz) whipped cream into ⅓ of the raspberry mixture, and fold the remaining cream into the other ⅔ of the raspberry mixture. Freeze as described above.

Nutrition information
Kcal 433; kj 1801; Protein 4.4 g;
Carbohydrates 24.8 g; Sugar 24.5 g;
Total Fat 35.9 g; Saturated Fat 21.8 g;
Fibre 2.1 g; Sodium 0.048 g

Ideal for a pool party!

Desserts

Chocolate Pistachio Cookies

Ingredients:

For the base:

200 g | 7 oz | 1¾ cups plain (all-purpose) flour
1 pinch salt
60 g | 2 oz | ¼ cup white (granulated) sugar
100 g | 3½ oz | ½ cup butter, softened
1 egg, beaten

For the topping:

160 mL | 6 fl oz | ⅔ cup cream, 30% fat
500 g | 18 oz plain (dark) chocolate, 70% cocoa solids, chopped
1 tsp almond extract
150 g | 5 oz | 1 cup pistachio nuts, roughly chopped

Method:

1 Heat the oven to 200°C (180° fan/400°F/gas 6). Grease a 10 cm x 25 cm (4 x 10 in) baking tin.

2 Mix together the flour, salt and sugar in a mixing bowl. Knead in the butter, then beat in the egg to form a dough. Roll out to fit the tin. Put the base in the tin and prick several times with a fork.

3 Bake for 25 minutes, until lightly golden. Remove from the oven and cool in the tin.

4 For the topping: bring the cream to a boil in a pan and slowly pour onto the chocolate. Leave to stand for 5 minutes, then stir in the almond extract until the mixture is smooth and the chocolate has completely melted. Stir in the pistachios.

5 Spread evenly on the base and chill for at least 4 hours. Cut into slices to serve.

Nutrition information
Kcal 569; kj 2379; Protein 8.6 g;
Carbohydrates 56.7 g; Sugar 40.6 g;
Total Fat 35.2 g; Saturated Fat 17 g;
Fibre 3.8 g; Sodium 0.164 g

Replace the almond extract with 1 tsp vanilla extract.

Instead of pistachios try chopped hazelnuts, Brazils or walnuts.

Desserts

Marshmallow Choc-Chip Cookies

Ingredients:

55 g | 2 oz | ¼ cup butter, melted
1½ tbsp golden (corn) syrup
100 g | 3½ oz | ½ cup white
    (granulated) sugar
1 egg yolk
175 g | 6 oz | 1½ cups plain
    (all-purpose) flour
1 tsp baking powder
1 good pinch ground ginger
1 good pinch ground cinnamon
1 good pinch ground mixed spice
1 pinch salt
55 g | 2 oz | ¾ cup chocolate chips

To decorate:
mini marshmallows
chocolate chips

Method:

1 Heat the oven to 180°C (160° fan/350°F/gas 4). Line 2 large baking trays (sheets) with non-stick baking paper.

2 Mix together the butter, syrup, sugar and egg yolk in a mixing bowl.

3 Sift in the flour, baking powder, spices and salt and work to a dough. Knead in the chocolate chips.

4 Put teaspoonfuls of the mixture on the baking trays, leaving plenty of space between them. Bake for 12–15 minutes until golden.

5 Halfway through the baking time, gently press mini marshmallows and chocolate chips into the top of the cookies and bake until done. Cool on the baking trays for a few minutes, then place on a wire rack to cool completely.

Nutrition information
Kcal 122; kj 516; Protein 1.5 g;
Carbohydrates 21.3 g; Sugar 13.8 g;
Total Fat 4.1 g; Saturated Fat 2.4 g;
Fibre 0.5 g

The cookies will spread as they cook, so they need to be spaced well apart on the baking tray.

Use white chocolate chips instead of plain or milk chocolate for a change.

Baked Goods

Butterfly Buns

Ingredients:

For the cakes:
125 g | 4½ oz | ½ cup butter
120 g | 4 oz | ½ cup white (granulated) sugar
2 eggs
200 g | 7 oz | 1 cup quark, 40% fat
250 g | 9 oz | 2¼ cups plain (all-purpose) flour
3 tsp baking powder
300 g | 11 oz | 1¼ cups bottled morello cherries, drained

To decorate:
2 sheets red gelatine
5 tbsp icing (confectioner's) sugar
150 g | 5 oz | ¾ cup quark, 40% fat
24 small sponge cookies, ready-made

Method:

1 Heat the oven to 180° C (160° C fan/375° F/gas 5). Place paper cases in 2 x 12 bun or cupcake tins.

2 Beat the butter with the sugar until pale and fluffy. Add the eggs and quark alternately.

3 Sift in the flour and baking powder and quickly beat until all the ingredients are moist. Mix half of the cherries into the mixture, reserving the rest for the decoration.

4 Spoon into the paper cases. Bake for 15–17 minutes. Test with a skewer or wooden cocktail stick – If it comes out clean, the buns are cooked. Cool in the tins for 5 minutes, then place on a wire rack to cool completely.

5 To decorate: soften the gelatine in cold water.

6 Puree the reserved cherries with a hand-held mixer. Squeeze out the gelatine and warm gently in a small saucepan with 2 tablespoons cherry puree.

7 Remove from the heat and stir in the remaining puree. Stir in 1 tablespoon icing (confectioner's) sugar and the quark.

8 Spread the cherry quark on the buns. Halve the cookies and arrange 2 halves on each bun to resemble butterfly wings. Sift over the remaining icing sugar.

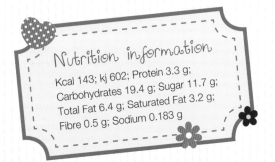

Nutrition information

Kcal 143; kj 602; Protein 3.3 g;
Carbohydrates 19.4 g; Sugar 11.7 g;
Total Fat 6.4 g; Saturated Fat 3.2 g;
Fibre 0.5 g; Sodium 0.183 g

If you can't find quark, try using fromage blanc or equal parts cream cheese and thickened (whipping) cream blended together.

Baked Goods

Pink Coconut Squares

Ingredients:

For the cake:
340 g | 12 oz | 1½ cups butter
265 g | 9 oz | 1¼ cups caster (berry) sugar
3 eggs, beaten
135 mL | 5 fl oz | 9 tbsp milk
1 tsp vanilla extract
340 g | 12 oz | 3¼ cups self-raising flour

For the icing (frosting):
125 g | 4½ oz | 1 cup raspberries
150–200 mL | 5–7 fl oz | ⅔ – ⅞ cup boiling water
600 g | 21 oz | 6 cups icing (confectioner's) sugar
few drops of pink food colouring

To decorate:
350 g | 12 oz | 4 cups desiccated (fine) coconut

Method:

1 Heat the oven to 160°C (140° fan/325°F/gas 3). Grease and line a 4 cm (1½ in) deep baking tin, 22 x 33 cm (9 x 11 in) with non-stick baking paper.

2 Beat the butter and sugar in a mixing bowl until thick and creamy.

3 Gradually beat in the eggs a little at a time. Stir in the milk and vanilla. Gently fold in the flour until incorporated.

4 Pour the mixture into the tin and smooth the top. Bake for 25–30 minutes, until golden and springy to the touch. Cool in the tin for 5 minutes, then place on a wire rack to cool completely.

5 Trim the edges off the cake and cut into 24 squares.

6 For the icing (frosting): crush the raspberries in a bowl with a fork, stir in 2 tablespoons boiling water and allow to cool for 5 minutes.

7 Sieve the raspberry mixture into a bowl, discarding the solids.

8 Sift the icing (confectioner's) sugar into a bowl. Whisk in the raspberry liquid and enough boiling water to form a smooth thick-coating icing. Stir in the food colouring.

9 Spread the coconut over the base of a tray.

10 Dip 1 cake square at a time into the icing, turning quickly to coat and allowing the excess to drip back into the bowl.

11 Roll in coconut and place on a wire rack to set.

Nutrition information

Kcal 396; kj 1661; Protein 3.2 g;
Carbohydrates 50 g; Sugar 39.2 g;
Total Fat 21.8 g; Saturated Fat 15.5 g;
Fibre 3.4 g; Sodium 0.156 g

Stir in the flour gently (don't beat) with a metal spoon. Overworking the mixture results in a leathery sponge.

Baked Goods

Vanilla Cupcakes

Ingredients:

For the cupcakes:
110 g | 4 oz | ½ cup butter
110 g | 4 oz | ½ cup white (granulated) sugar
1 tsp vanilla extract
2 eggs, beaten
110 g | 4 oz | 1 cup self-raising flour
½ tsp baking powder

For the topping:
300 mL | 11 fl oz | 1⅓ cups cream, 48% fat
1 tsp vanilla extract
2 tsp icing (confectioner's) sugar

To decorate:
pink flowers

Method:

1 For the cupcakes: heat the oven to 180°C (160° fan/ 350°F/gas 4). Place paper cases in a 10-hole bun or cupcake tin.

2 Beat the butter and sugar in a mixing bowl until light and creamy. Beat in the vanilla.

3 Add the eggs gradually, beating well. Sift in the flour and baking powder and gently fold into the mixture.

4 Spoon the mixture into the paper cases and bake for about 20 minutes, until golden and springy to the touch. Cool in the tin for a few minutes, then place on a wire rack to cool completely.

5 For the topping: whisk together the cream, vanilla and icing (confectioner's) sugar into soft peaks that hold their shape.

6 Spoon into a piping bag with a plain nozzle and pipe on top of the cakes.

7 Decorate with flowers.

Omit the vanilla extract from the cakes and add the finely grated zest of an orange or lemon.

Nutrition information
Kcal 330; kj 1371; Protein 2.8 g;
Carbohydrates 21.6 g; Sugar 13.3 g;
Total Fat 26.4 g; Saturated Fat 16.1 g;
Fibre 0.5 g; Sodium 0.175 g

Be careful not to over-whisk the cream topping. It should be thick but not stiff.

Raspberry Butter Cookies

Ingredients:

For the dough:
400 g | 14 oz | 3½ cups plain (all-purpose) flour
125 g | 4½ oz | ⅔ cup white (granulated) sugar
1–2 tsp vanilla extract
250 g | 9 oz | 1 cup butter
4 egg yolks

For the topping:
250 g | 9 oz | 1 cup raspberry jam (jelly)
200 g | 7 oz | 1½ cups raspberries

Method:

1 Combine all the dough ingredients and quickly knead to a smooth dough. Add a little ice-cold water if the dough is too crumbly. Wrap in cling film and chill for at least 1 hour.

2 Heat the oven to 180°C (160°C fan/375°F/gas 5). Line a large baking tray (sheet) with non-stick baking paper.

3 Divide the dough into 2 portions and roll each portion into a sausage about 4 cm (1½ in) diameter. Cut into slices about 1 cm (½ in) thick and flatten slightly. Put onto the baking tray and bake for 15–20 minutes, until nicely browned.

4 Place on a wire rack to cool completely. Push the raspberry jam (jelly) through a sieve and put a blob of jam on top of each cookie. Add 2 raspberries to each and press on lightly.

You can use strawberries and strawberry jam (jelly) instead of raspberries.

Nutrition information
Kcal 102; kj 427; Protein 1.5 g;
Carbohydrates 12.5 g; Sugar 6.4 g;
Total Fat 5.4 g; Saturated Fat 3 g;
Fibre 0.5 g; Sodium 0.033 g

Berry Crostata

Ingredients:

For the pastry:

250 g | 9 oz | 2¼ cups plain (all-purpose) flour
1 pinch salt
150 g | 5 oz | ⅔ cup butter, diced
50 g | 1¾ oz | ¼ cup white (granulated) sugar
1 egg, beaten
2–3 tbsp cold water

For the filling:

200 g | 7 oz | 1½ cups raspberries
100 g | 3½ oz | ½ cup white (granulated) sugar
3 eggs
55 g | 2 oz | ¼ cup butter
4 tbsp cream, 48% fat
200 g | 7 oz | 1½ cups mixed berries
icing (confectioner's) sugar, for dusting

Method:

1 For the pastry: sift the flour and salt into a bowl. Rub in the butter until the mixture resembles breadcrumbs. Add the sugar.

2 Make a well in the centre of the mixture, add the egg and a little cold water and mix to a dough. Form into a ball, wrap in cling film and chill for 30 minutes.

3 For the filling: puree the raspberries in a food processor or blender and push through a sieve. Weigh out 125 g (4.5 oz) of the puree.

4 Mix the raspberry puree with the sugar, eggs, butter and cream. Put into a heatproof bowl over a pan of simmering (not boiling) water. Stir until it thickens, but don't allow to become too hot or boil. Set aside to cool.

5 Heat the oven to 180°C (160° fan/350°F/gas 4). Grease a 23 cm (9 in) square tart tin with a removable base.

6 Roll out the pastry on a floured surface and use to line the tart tin. Trim the dough overhang to 1 cm (½ in). Fold the overhang in; press firmly, forming double-thick sides. Cover with non-stick baking paper and baking beads or baking beans, then bake for 10 minutes. Remove the beans and paper and bake for a further 10 minutes. Set aside to cool in the tin.

7 Reduce the oven temperature to 160°C (140° fan/325°F/gas 3).

8 Spread the berry cream in the pastry case and bake for a further 25 minutes. Leave to cool completely.

9 Remove from the tin and place the mixed berries on top of the tart. Serve dusted with icing (confectioner's) sugar.

Nutrition information

Kcal 615; kj 2563; Protein 7.5 g;
Carbohydrates 51.4 g; Sugar 32.3 g;
Total Fat 43.6 g; Saturated Fat 22.5 g;
Fibre 2.7 g; Sodium 0.425 g

Don't let the raspberry cream mixture become too hot in the heat-proof bowl, or the mixture will curdle.

It's important to let the pastry case cool before spreading with the berry cream filling.

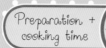
Love-Heart Cookies

Ingredients:

For the cookies:
225 g | 8 oz | 1 cup unsalted butter
100 g | 3½ oz | ½ cup caster
　(berry) sugar
200 g | 7 oz | 1¾ cups plain
　(all-purpose) flour
100 g | 3½ oz | ¾ cup ground almonds
150 g | 5 oz | ½ cup seedless
　raspberry jam (jelly)

To decorate:
2–3 tbsp seedless raspberry jam (jelly)
2 tsp boiling water
coloured sprinkles

Method:

1 Beat the butter in a mixing bowl until soft. Add the sugar, flour and ground almonds and mix with your hands to form a dough.

2 Knead the dough lightly until smooth. Wrap in cling film and chill for 1 hour.

3 Heat the oven to 150°C (130° fan/300°F/gas 2). Line 2 large baking trays (sheets) with non-stick baking paper.

4 Roll out the dough on a lightly floured surface, about 5 mm (¼ in) thick. Cut into heart shapes using a heart-shaped cookie cutter and place on the baking trays.

5 Bake for about 20 minutes until lightly golden. Cool on the baking trays for a few minutes, then place on a wire rack to cool completely.

6 Sandwich the biscuits together with the jam (jelly).

7 To decorate: heat the jam with the hot water until melted. Brush over the top of each heart and sprinkle with the coloured sprinkles.

Nutrition information
Kcal 173; kj 726; Protein 1.7 g;
Carbohydrates 21.1 g; Sugar 14.9 g;
Total Fat 9.7 g; Saturated Fat 4.9 g;
Fibre 0.3 g; Sodium 0.052 g

You can use any type of jam (jelly) to vary the flavour, such as blackcurrant, strawberry or plum.

Baked Goods

Double-Choc Cupcakes

Ingredients:

For the cupcakes:
110 g | 4 oz | ½ cup butter, softened
110 g | 4 oz | ¾ cup white (granulated) sugar
80 g | 3 oz | ¾ cup self-raising flour
25 g | 1 oz | ¼ cup cocoa powder
1 pinch baking powder
2 eggs

For the chocolate ganache topping:
150 mL | 5 fl oz | ⅔ cup cream, 48% fat
350 g | 12 oz plain (dark) chocolate, 60% cocoa solids, chopped
55 g | 2 oz | ¼ cup unsalted butter

To decorate:
pink paper flowers

Method:

1 For the cupcakes: heat the oven to 190°C (170° fan/ 375°F/gas 5). Place 12 paper cases in a 12-hole bun or cupcake tin.

2 Whisk together the butter, sugar, flour, cocoa, baking powder and eggs until smooth and blended.

3 Spoon into the paper cases and bake for about 15 minutes until well risen and firm to the touch. Cool in the tin for 5 minutes, then place on a wire rack to cool completely.

4 For the chocolate ganache: heat the cream to a boil in a pan. Remove from the heat and add the chocolate. Leave to stand for 5 minutes, then stir until the chocolate has melted. Add the butter and stir until the mixture is smooth and glossy. Chill until firm, but not hard.

5 Put the mixture into a piping bag and pipe swirls on top of the cakes. Decorate with flowers.

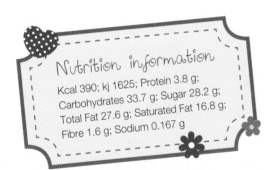

Nutrition information
Kcal 390; kj 1625; Protein 3.8 g;
Carbohydrates 33.7 g; Sugar 28.2 g;
Total Fat 27.6 g; Saturated Fat 16.8 g;
Fibre 1.6 g; Sodium 0.167 g

Use milk chocolate or white chocolate instead of plain chocolate.

Baked Goods

Raspberry Coconut Cake

Ingredients:

For the cake:
4 eggs, separated
200 g | 7 oz | 1 cup white (granulated) sugar
50 g | 1¾ oz | ¾ cup desiccated (fine) coconut
250 g | 9 oz | 2¼ cups plain (all-purpose) flour
1 tsp baking powder
120 g | 4 oz | ½ cup butter, melted

For the topping:
200 g | 7 oz | 1 cup raspberries
2 tbsp water
2 tbsp icing (confectioner's) sugar
300 mL | 11 fl oz | 1⅓ cups cream, 48% fat
1 tbsp coconut syrup

To decorate:
shaved coconut
icing (confectioner's) sugar

Method:

1 Heat the oven to 160°C (140° fan/325°F/gas 3). Grease a 20 cm (8 in) springform deep cake tin and line the base with non-stick baking paper.

2 Whisk the egg whites with 2 tablespoons sugar until stiff and fold in the coconut.

3 Whisk the egg yolks with the remaining sugar until creamy. Sift in the flour and baking powder and gently stir into the mixture. Fold in the coconut mixture until blended, followed by the melted butter.

4 Spoon into the tin and bake for about 1 hour until cooked through. Insert a skewer into the centre of the cake; it will come out clean when the cake is cooked. Cool in the tin for 5 minutes, then place on a wire rack to cool completely.

5 Put half the raspberries into a pan with the water. Bring to a boil, then simmer gently until soft. Sieve the raspberries into a bowl and stir in 1 tablespoon icing (confectioner's) sugar.

6 Whisk the cream with the remaining icing sugar until stiff, then whisk in the syrup.

7 Spoon the whipped cream on top of the cake and decorate with the remaining raspberries and the raspberry puree. Arrange the shaved coconut on top and sift over a little icing sugar.

Nutrition information
Kcal 614; kj 2562; Protein 6.3 g;
Carbohydrates 56.2 g; Sugar 32.1 g;
Total Fat 42.1 g; Saturated Fat 27.5 g;
Fibre 4.4 g; Sodium 0.182 g

Try this with strawberries or blueberries instead of raspberries.

Baked Goods

Chocolate and Buttercream Cupcakes

Ingredients:

For the cupcakes:
150 g | 5 oz | ⅔ cup butter, softened
150 g | 5 oz | ¾ cup caster
　(berry) sugar
175 g | 6 oz | 1½ cups self-raising flour
3 eggs, beaten
2 tbsp cocoa powder

For the buttercream:
120 g | 4 oz | ½ cup unsalted butter
200 g | 7 oz | 2 cups icing
　(confectioner's) sugar
few drops of pink food colouring
½ tsp rosewater

For the decoration:
white sugar sprinkles

Method:

1 For the cupcakes: heat the oven to 190°C (170° fan/ 375°F/gas 5). Place paper cases in a 12-hole bun or cupcake tin.

2 Place all the ingredients in a mixing bowl and whisk with an electric whisk until blended. Alternatively beat well with a wooden spoon.

3 Spoon the mixture into the paper cases and bake for 20–25 minutes until springy to the touch. Remove from the tin and place on a wire rack to cool completely.

4 For the buttercream: beat the butter in a bowl until soft.

5 Sift in the icing (confectioner's) sugar and beat well. Stir in the pink food colouring and rosewater.

6 Spoon into a piping bag. Pipe swirls on each cake. Scatter with sugar sprinkles.

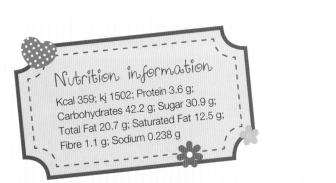

Nutrition information
Kcal 359; kj 1502; Protein 3.6 g;
Carbohydrates 42.2 g; Sugar 30.9 g;
Total Fat 20.7 g; Saturated Fat 12.5 g;
Fibre 1.1 g; Sodium 0.238 g

If you don't want to pipe the buttercream, just spoon it on top of the cakes.

Instead of sugar sprinkles try crystallised rose petals or grated chocolate.

Baked Goods

Sliders

Ingredients:

500 g | 18 oz minced (ground) beef
1 small onion, finely chopped
salt and freshly ground black pepper
8 mini bread rolls
2 cherry tomatoes, sliced
lettuce
8 slices continental (English) cucumber
8 squares cheddar cheese, sliced

Method:

1 Heat the grill (broiler).

2 Place the minced (ground) beef in a mixing bowl with the onion. Season well with salt and pepper and mix by hand until combined.

3 Shape the mixture into 8 mini burgers.

4 Grill (broil) for about 3 minutes on each side, until cooked through.

5 Cut open the bread rolls and place the tomatoes, lettuce and cucumber on the base of each roll. Put the burgers on top, and top with a cheese square. Place the bread roll tops on the cheese and serve immediately.

Nutrition information
Kcal 316; kj 1324; Protein 19.9 g;
Carbohydrates 27.4 g; Sugar 3.9 g;
Total Fat 14.8 g; Saturated Fat 6.7 g;
Fibre 2.1 g; Sodium 0.381 g

Don't use extra-lean mince as the fat is needed to help bind the burgers and keep them juicy.

Pizza Muffins

Ingredients:

300 g | 11 oz | 2¾ cups plain (all-purpose) flour
1 tbsp baking powder
1 pinch mustard powder
1 tsp salt
freshly ground black pepper
2 tsp snipped chives
1 large egg
100 g | 3½ oz soft cheese with herbs
200 mL | 7 fl oz | ⅞ cup milk
2 tomatoes, diced
2 spring onions (scallions), thinly sliced
55 g | 2 oz cooked ham, diced
75 g | 2½ oz cheddar cheese, grated

Method:

1 Heat the oven to 180°C (160° fan/350°F/gas 4). Line a 12-hole muffin tin with paper cases.

2 Sift the flour, baking powder and mustard powder into a mixing bowl, and add the salt, freshly ground black pepper and chives.

3 Whisk together the egg, soft cheese and milk until smooth. Stir in the tomatoes, spring onions (scallions) and ham.

4 Pour the wet ingredients into the dry ingredients, and mix gently until just incorporated. The mixture will be slightly lumpy.

5 Spoon into the greased paper cases and sprinkle the top of each muffin with grated cheese. Bake for about 20 minutes, until the muffins are golden and firm to the touch. Serve warm.

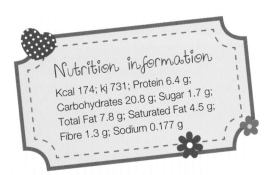

Nutrition information

Kcal 174; kj 731; Protein 6.4 g;
Carbohydrates 20.8 g; Sugar 1.7 g;
Total Fat 7.8 g; Saturated Fat 4.5 g;
Fibre 1.3 g; Sodium 0.177 g

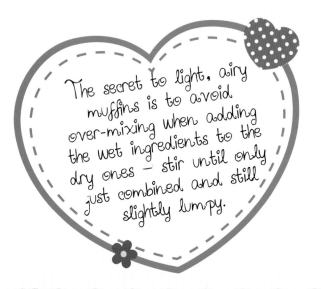

The secret to light, airy muffins is to avoid over-mixing when adding the wet ingredients to the dry ones — stir until only just combined and still slightly lumpy.

Chicken Nuggets

Ingredients:

100 mL | 3½ fl oz | 7 tbsp water
55 g | 2 oz | ½ cup plain (all-purpose)
    flour, plus 2 tbsp
1 egg
½ tsp salt
½ tsp onion salt
370 g | 13 oz chicken breast,
    cut into chunks
sunflower oil for deep frying

To serve:
tomato sauce (ketchup)

Method:

1 Whisk together the water, 55 g flour, egg, salt and onion salt in a mixing bowl until smooth.

2 Toss the chicken pieces in the remaining 2 tablespoons flour until coated, then stir into the batter.

3 Heat the oil in a deep fryer or pan. Carefully drop the chicken pieces in batches into the hot oil and cook for about 7 minutes until golden and crisp. Keep warm while you cook the remaining chicken.

4 Drain on absorbent kitchen paper and serve with tomato sauce (ketchup).

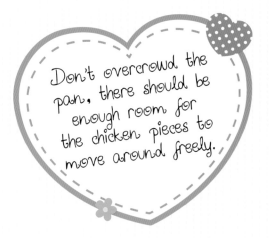

Don't overcrowd the pan, there should be enough room for the chicken pieces to move around freely.

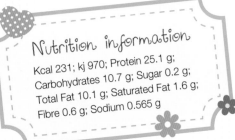

Nutrition information
Kcal 231; kj 970; Protein 25.1 g;
Carbohydrates 10.7 g; Sugar 0.2 g;
Total Fat 10.1 g; Saturated Fat 1.6 g;
Fibre 0.6 g; Sodium 0.565 g

Falafel

Ingredients:

800 g | 28 oz canned chickpeas (garbanzo beans), rinsed and drained
2 cloves garlic, chopped
1 small onion, chopped
2 tsp ground cumin
2 tsp ground coriander
1 handful fresh coriander (cilantro) leaves, chopped
1 tsp harissa paste or chilli powder
4 tbsp plain (all-purpose) flour
½ tsp salt
7–8 tbsp sesame seeds
4–5 tbsp sunflower oil

To garnish:
basil

Method:

1 Put all the ingredients except the sesame seeds and oil into a food processor or blender and blend until fairly smooth. Shape into 8 patties with your hands.

2 Sprinkle the sesame seeds onto a plate and roll the patties in the sesame seeds to coat.

3 Heat the oil in a large frying pan (skillet), add the patties, then fry for 3 minutes on each side until lightly golden.

4 Drain on absorbent kitchen paper and serve garnished with basil.

Use mint or parsley instead of chopped coriander (cilantro) for a different flavour.

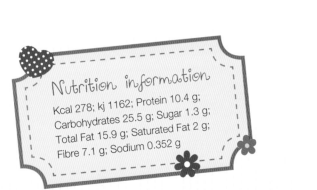

Nutrition information
Kcal 278; kj 1162; Protein 10.4 g;
Carbohydrates 25.5 g; Sugar 1.3 g;
Total Fat 15.9 g; Saturated Fat 2 g;
Fibre 7.1 g; Sodium 0.352 g

Party Food

Herbed Chicken Fillets

Ingredients:

4 slices bread, made into breadcrumbs
2 tbsp chopped mixed herbs, e.g.
   parsley, rosemary, thyme
salt and pepper
3 skinless boneless chicken breasts,
   cut into strips
1 egg, beaten

Method:

1 Heat the oven to 200°C (180° fan/400°F/gas 6). Grease a baking tray (sheet).

2 Spread the breadcrumbs on the baking tray. Bake for 15 minutes until crisp and tip into a bowl. Re-grease the baking tray.

3 Mix together the breadcrumbs, herbs and salt and pepper to taste and mix well.

4 Dip the chicken strips in the beaten egg then press the chicken into the breadcrumbs, coating all sides. Place on the baking tray, placing any excess crumbs on top.

5 Bake for 15–20 minutes until thoroughly cooked. Check by inserting a knife into the meat. The juices should run clear when fully cooked.

6 Eat hot or cold.

Nutrition information

Kcal 193; kj 818; Protein 30.6 g;
Carbohydrates 11.6 g; Sugar 0.9 g;
Total Fat 3.1 g; Saturated Fat 0.8 g;
Fibre 0.7 g; Sodium 0.201 g

Vary the flavour by using different herbs such as basil or mint.

Try turkey breasts instead of chicken.

Party Food

Nachos with Salsa and Guacamole

Ingredients:

For the salsa:
6 large tomatoes, deseeded and chopped
2 red chillies, deseeded and
    finely chopped
1 small onion, finely sliced
1–2 dashes Tabasco (hot) sauce
2 cloves garlic, finely chopped
1 large lime, juice
1 tbsp chopped coriander (cilantro)
1 tbsp extra virgin olive oil
salt, to taste

For the guacamole:
3 mild chillies, finely chopped
1 tbsp finely chopped coriander
    (cilantro)
salt, to taste
1 onion, finely chopped
½ lime, juice
3 ripe avocados

For the nachos:
400 g | 14 oz corn (tortilla) chips
200 g | 7 oz | 2 cups grated
    cheddar cheese

To garnish:
coriander (cilantro)

Method:

1 For the salsa: mix together all the ingredients until well combined. Leave to stand for 10 minutes.

2 For the guacamole: pound the chillies, coriander (cilantro), salt and onion to a fine paste in a pestle and mortar or blender. Add the lime juice to make a loose smooth mixture.

3 Put the avocado flesh into a bowl and mash until smooth. Add the pounded mixture and stir well. Cover and chill for 10 minutes.

4 For the nachos: heat the oven to 220°C (200° fan/425°F/gas 7).

5 Put the corn (tortilla) chips into a large ovenproof dish. Scatter over half the salsa and all the grated cheese. Cook for about 5 minutes, until the cheese has melted.

6 Put the remaining salsa in a serving bowl. Put the guacamole in a serving bowl. Serve with the nachos and garnish with coriander.

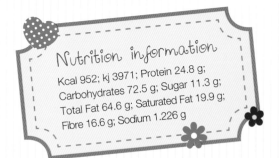

Nutrition information
Kcal 952; kj 3971; Protein 24.8 g;
Carbohydrates 72.5 g; Sugar 11.3 g;
Total Fat 64.6 g; Saturated Fat 19.9 g;
Fibre 16.6 g; Sodium 1.226 g

Make sure you use ripe avocados for the guacamole. Test by squeezing the end, which should yield to slight pressure.

Party Food

Baked Potato Wedges with Dip

Ingredients:

For the potato wedges:
3 medium baking potatoes
1–2 tbsp olive oil
2 tsp crushed garlic
2 tsp paprika
2 tsp ground cumin
1 tsp ground black pepper

To garnish:
flat-leaf parsley

For the dip:
8 tbsp cream cheese
8 tbsp soured cream
1 clove garlic, crushed
1 tsp onion salt
ground white pepper
3 tsp snipped chives

Method:

1 Heat the oven to 200°C (180° fan/400°F/gas 6). Grease a baking tray (sheet).

2 Cut each potato into 8 wedges. Put into a pan of boiling salted water and cook for 8 minutes. Drain and set aside to cool until warm.

3 Mix together the remaining ingredients (not those for the dip) in a bowl. Coat the potato wedges in the spicy paste and place on the baking tray, skin side down.

4 Bake the potatoes for 25 minutes, until brown and crisp. Put into a serving bowl and garnish with parsley.

5 For the dip: beat together all the ingredients, except the chives. Put into a serving bowl and sprinkle with the chives.

Nutrition information
Kcal 492; kj 2052; Protein 7.7 g;
Carbohydrates 44.4 g; Sugar 3.2 g;
Total Fat 32.7 g; Saturated Fat 17.7 g;
Fibre 4.9 g; Sodium 0.546 g

To give the dip an extra kick use cayenne pepper instead of white pepper.

Berry Domes

Ingredients:

5 leaves gelatine
550 mL | 19 fl oz | 2⅓ cups strawberry
    or cranberry cordial (concentrate)
50 mL | 1¾ fl oz | 10 tsp water
200 g | 7 oz | 2 cups mixed raspberries
    and blueberries

Method:

1 Soak the gelatine leaves for 3–4 minutes in just enough cold water to cover.

2 Heat 100 mL (3 fl oz) of the cordial (concentrate) in a pan until hot, but not boiling. Remove from the heat.

3 Squeeze out the excess water from the gelatine. Stir the gelatine into the warm cordial until completely dissolved.

4 Pour into a measuring jug and add the water up to 600 mL (20 fl oz) and stir well.

5 Divide the fruit among 4 individual pudding basins or moulds and pour in the cordial mixture. Chill for 2–3 hours until firm.

6 Dip the base of the moulds into hot water and unmould the jellies (jellos) onto serving plates.

Note: at step 4 you must add the remaining cordial to the dissolved gelatine and not vice versa, or the gelatine will become stringy.

Nutrition information

Kcal 157; kj 671; Protein 2.8 g;
Carbohydrates 38.8 g; Sugar 37.5 g;
Total Fat 0.1 g; Saturated Fat trace;
Fibre 1.3 g; Sodium 0.064 g

For a vegetarian version, use agar agar or Vege-Gel instead of gelatine.

Party Food

Melon Ball Skewers

Ingredients:

½ cantaloupe melon, seeds removed
½ honeydew (or charentais) melon, seeds removed
¼ watermelon, seeds removed
50 mL | 1¾ fl oz | 10 tsp lemon juice
2–3 tbsp white (granulated) sugar

Method:

1 Line a large tray with non-stick baking paper.

2 Using a melon baller, scoop out balls from the melon flesh.

3 Mix the lemon juice and sugar with a little water and gently stir in the melon balls until coated with sugar.

4 Thread the melon balls (alternating the colours) on wooden skewers and place on the tray. Freeze for at least 3 hours.

5 Remove from the freezer about 5 minutes before serving and arrange on a serving plate.

Puree the rest of the melon flesh and mix with well-chilled buttermilk for a refreshing summer drink.

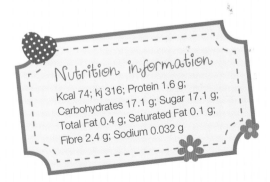

Nutrition information

Kcal 74; kj 316; Protein 1.6 g;
Carbohydrates 17.1 g; Sugar 17.1 g;
Total Fat 0.4 g; Saturated Fat 0.1 g;
Fibre 2.4 g; Sodium 0.032 g

Homemade Lemonade

Ingredients:

4 unwaxed lemons
225 g | 8 oz | 1 cup white (granulated) sugar
1⅘ L (2 qt) boiling water

To decorate:
lime slices

Method:

1 Using a vegetable peeler, thinly pare the rind from the lemons, and then squeeze out the juice.

2 Put the lemon rind and sugar into a bowl and pour over the boiling water. Stir to dissolve the sugar, cover and leave for 24 hours until completely cold.

3 Add the lemon juice (add more sugar if you wish) and strain into a jug. Chill until ready to serve and decorate with lime slices.

Always use unwaxed (preferably organic) lemons, as waxed lemons contain a fungicide.

Nutrition information

Kcal 112; kj 480; Protein 0.1 g;
Carbohydrates 29.9 g; Sugar 29.9 g;
Total Fat trace; Saturated Fat trace;
Fibre trace; Sodium 0.002 g

Perfect for a lemonade stand!

Party Food

Shortbread S'mores

Ingredients:

110 g | 4 oz | ½ cup unsalted butter
55 g | 2 oz | ¼ cup white (granulated) sugar
1 lemon, grated zest
175 g | 6 oz | 1½ cups plain (all-purpose) flour
1 pinch salt
6 tbsp chocolate spread
12 white marshmallows

Method:

1 Beat the butter, sugar and lemon zest in a mixing bowl until soft and creamy.

2 Sift in the flour and salt and mix to a dough. Shape the dough into a log about 5 cm (2 in) wide and wrap in cling film. Chill for 1 hour.

3 Heat the oven to 160°C (140° fan/325°F/gas 3). Line a baking tray (sheet) with non-stick baking paper.

4 Cut the log with a sharp knife into 12 rounds and place on the baking tray. Bake for 18–20 minutes, until golden brown around the edges. Cool on the baking tray for 5 minutes, then place on a wire rack to cool completely.

5 Heat the grill (broiler). Line the grill tray with non-stick baking paper.

6 Toast the marshmallows under the grill until lightly golden and starting to melt.

7 Spoon a little chocolate spread on each shortbread round and place a marshmallow on top.

Nutrition information

Kcal 209; kj 876; Protein 2 g;
Carbohydrates 26.1 g; Sugar 14 g;
Total Fat 11.5 g; Saturated Fat 4.8 g;
Fibre 0.6 g; Sodium 0.058 g

Watch the marshmallows carefully, as they burn easily.

Sleepover Treats

Homemade Popcorn

Ingredients:

1½ tbsp sunflower oil
100 g | 3½ oz popping corn
salt or white (granulated) sugar

Method:

1 Heat the oil in a large pan until very hot, but not smoking.

2 Tip in the popping corn and quickly cover with a tight-fitting lid and wait for the corn to start popping.

3 Shake the pan over a low-medium heat. When the popping has ceased, remove the lid and sprinkle with salt or sugar, then pour into a large bowl.

For sweet buttery popcorn, toss the hot freshly popped corn in 55 g (2 oz) butter melted with 1 tablespoon honey until coated.

Nutrition information

Kcal 166; kj 691; Protein 1.6 g;
Carbohydrates 12.2 g; Sugar 0.3 g;
Total Fat 12.7 g; Saturated Fat 1.3 g;
Fibre trace; Sodium 0.787 g (salted)

Every movie
night needs
popcorn!

Sleepover Treats

Chocolate-Dipped Marshmallows

Ingredients:

12 marshmallows
100 g | 3½ oz plain (dark) chocolate,
   70% cocoa solids
sugar pearls

Method:

1 Melt the chocolate in a heatproof bowl over a pan of simmering (not boiling) water. Remove from the heat and allow to cool and thicken slightly.

2 Line a tray with non-stick baking paper.

3 Put the marshmallows onto skewers or lollipop sticks and dip halfway in the chocolate, then dip into the sugar pearls. Place on the tray to set.

These look great with pink marshmallows, white chocolate, and coloured sugar pearls.

Nutrition information

Kcal 77; kj 324; Protein 0.8 g;
Carbohydrates 14 g; Sugar 12.1 g;
Total Fat 2.3 g; Saturated Fat 1.4 g;
Fibre 0.3 g; Sodium 0.004 g

You can use milk chocolate instead of plain chocolate.

Sleepover Treats

Sweet and Salty Nuts

Ingredients:

200 g | 7 oz | 2 cups roughly chopped mixed nuts
2 tbsp white (granulated) sugar
¾ tsp salt
½ tsp ground cinnamon
⅛ tsp ground allspice
⅛ tsp cayenne pepper
1 tbsp water
2 tsp vanilla extract
1 tsp light brown sugar
1 tbsp sunflower oil

Method:

1 Heat the oven to 180°C (160° fan/350°F/gas 4). Line a large baking tray (sheet) with non-stick baking paper.

2 Spread the nuts on the baking tray and toast for about 6 minutes, until fragrant and lightly toasted.

3 Stir together the sugar, salt and spices in a mixing bowl.

4 Put the water, vanilla, brown sugar and oil into a pan and bring to a boil over a medium heat, whisking constantly.

5 Stir in the toasted nuts and continue to stir until the nuts are shiny and the liquid is absorbed.

6 Tip the glazed nuts into the mixing bowl and toss well to coat in the spices. Spread the coated nuts on the baking tray and return to the oven for a further 4 minutes. Leave to cool on the baking tray.

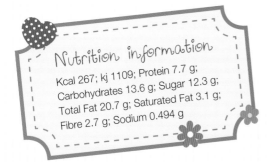

Nutrition information

Kcal 267; kj 1109; Protein 7.7 g;
Carbohydrates 13.6 g; Sugar 12.3 g;
Total Fat 20.7 g; Saturated Fat 3.1 g;
Fibre 2.7 g; Sodium 0.494 g

Instead of mixed nuts, use just pecans or walnuts.

Sleepover Treats

Hot Chocolate with Marshmallows

Ingredients:

600 mL | 21 fl oz | 2½ cups milk
140 mL | 5 fl oz | ⅝ cup cream,
   48% fat
100 g | 3½ oz plain (dark) chocolate,
   70% cocoa solids, broken
pink and white marshmallows

Method:

1 Put the milk, cream and chocolate into a pan. Bring to a boil over a low heat, whisking until smooth.

2 Pour into cups and place 2 marshmallows on top of each, to gently melt into the hot chocolate.

Try milk chocolate instead of plain chocolate.

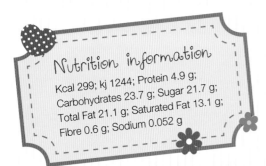

Nutrition information
Kcal 299; kj 1244; Protein 4.9 g;
Carbohydrates 23.7 g; Sugar 21.7 g;
Total Fat 21.1 g; Saturated Fat 13.1 g;
Fibre 0.6 g; Sodium 0.052 g

The perfect drink for your late-night secret chat!

Blueberry Pancakes

Ingredients:

200 g | 7 oz | 1¾ cups self-raising flour
1 tsp baking powder
1 pinch salt
1 egg
300 mL | 11 fl oz | 1⅓ cups milk
25 g | 1 oz | ⅛ cup butter, melted
150 g | 5 oz | 1 cup blueberries
butter for cooking
maple syrup

Method:

1 Mix together the flour, baking powder and salt in a mixing bowl.

2 Beat the egg with the milk, make a well in the centre of the dry ingredients and whisk in the milk mixture to make a thick, smooth batter.

3 Beat in the melted butter and gently stir in half the blueberries.

4 Heat a small knob of butter in a large frying pan (skillet). Drop large tablespoonfuls of the batter into the pan, about 7.5 cm (3 in) in diameter. Cook 3–4 pancakes at a time.

5 Cook for about 3 minutes until small bubbles appear on the surface of each pancake, then turn and cook the other side for a further 2–3 minutes until golden. Cover with non-stick baking paper to keep warm and repeat the process with the remaining batter.

6 Serve with the remaining blueberries and maple syrup.

Nutrition information

Kcal 140; kj 586; Protein 3.6 g;
Carbohydrates 18.8 g; Sugar 3.2 g;
Total Fat 6.1 g; Saturated Fat 3.5 g;
Fibre 1.1 g; Sodium 0.169 g

Instead of maple syrup you can serve the pancakes with golden (corn) syrup.

Sleepover Treats

French Toast

Ingredients:

4 eggs
200 mL | 7 fl oz | ⅞ cup milk
2 tbsp caster (berry) sugar
55–75 g | 2–2½ oz | ¼–⅓ cup butter
4–6 slices slightly stale bread
6 large strawberries, sliced
icing (confectioner's) sugar

Method:

1 Beat together the eggs, milk and sugar in a shallow bowl.

2 Heat a knob of the butter in a frying pan (skillet) until it foams.

3 Dip each slice of bread in the egg mixture, soaking both sides. Soak the bread in the mixture for a couple of seconds, turning over until each side is well coated.

4 Place 2 bread slices in the pan and cook on both sides until golden and crisp. Repeat with the remaining butter and soaked bread.

5 Cut the bread slices in half and place on serving plates. Top with the strawberries and sift over a little icing (confectioner's) sugar. Eat hot or warm.

For an extra-fruity flavour, add the grated zest of a lemon, lime or orange to the egg mixture before soaking the bread.

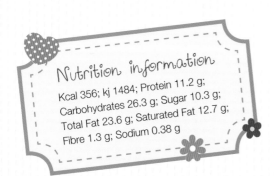

Nutrition information

Kcal 356; kj 1484; Protein 11.2 g;
Carbohydrates 26.3 g; Sugar 10.3 g;
Total Fat 23.6 g; Saturated Fat 12.7 g;
Fibre 1.3 g; Sodium 0.38 g

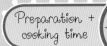

Boiled Egg and Soldiers

Ingredients:

4 eggs
2–3 slices toasted bread
butter

Method:

1 Bring a pan of water to a boil and carefully put in the eggs. Boil for 3 minutes (for soft-boiled) and remove from the pan.

2 Put the eggs into egg cups and slice off the tops.

3 Butter the toast, cut into 'soldiers' and serve with the eggs.

This recipe produces a soft-boiled egg with a runny yolk. For a firmer yolk, boil for 4–5 minutes in total.

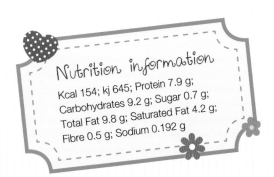

Nutrition information

Kcal 154; kj 645; Protein 7.9 g;
Carbohydrates 9.2 g; Sugar 0.7 g;
Total Fat 9.8 g; Saturated Fat 4.2 g;
Fibre 0.5 g; Sodium 0.192 g

Sleepover Treats

Berry Breakfast Smoothie

Ingredients:

150 mL | 5 fl oz | ⅔ cup plain yoghurt
2 very ripe bananas
300 g | 11 oz strawberries and
    raspberries, mixed
300 mL | 11 fl oz | 1⅓ cups milk

Method:

1 Put all the ingredients in a food processor and blend until smooth.

2 Pour into chilled glasses and serve immediately.

Use any combination of berries e.g. blueberries, cherries, redcurrants, as long as the weight totals 300 g (11 oz).

Nutrition information

Kcal 122; kj 514; Protein 5.7 g;
Carbohydrates 16.1 g; Sugar 15.5 g;
Total Fat 4.3 g; Saturated Fat 2.7 g;
Fibre 2.2 g; Sodium 0.066 g

Start your day with berry goodness!

Sleepover Treats

Banana Smoothie

Ingredients:

4 bananas, cut into chunks
1100 mL | 39 fl oz | 4½ cups milk
4 tbsp honey
6 ice cubes, crushed
1 tsp ground cinnamon
1 tsp ground cardamom

Method:

1 Put the bananas, milk, honey and ice into a blender and blend until smooth.

2 Pour into glasses and sprinkle with ground cinnamon and cardamom.

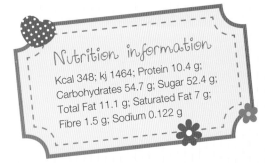

Nutrition information

Kcal 348; kj 1464; Protein 10.4 g;
Carbohydrates 54.7 g; Sugar 52.4 g;
Total Fat 11.1 g; Saturated Fat 7 g;
Fibre 1.5 g; Sodium 0.122 g

Swap sweets — replace the honey with maple syrup.

Sleepover Treats

Vegetable Wraps

Ingredients:

4–6 tortillas or bread wraps
4 tbsp cream cheese
2 carrots, cut into sticks
1 red onion, diced
½ small continental (English) cucumber,
    very thinly sliced
½ iceberg lettuce, shredded
1 tbsp finely chopped parsley
½ tbsp torn basil
salt and pepper
200 g | 7 oz cheddar cheese,
    cut into sticks

To garnish:
mint leaves

Method:

1 Spread the tortillas with the cream cheese.

2 Mix together the vegetables and herbs and season to taste with salt and pepper.

3 Divide the mixture between the wraps. Place the cheese sticks on top and roll up. Garnish with mint to serve.

Nutrition information
Kcal 372; kj 1554; Protein 14 g;
Carbohydrates 39 g; Sugar 8.8 g;
Total Fat 18.8 g; Saturated Fat 11.3 g;
Fibre 5.1 g; Sodium 0.426 g

Instead of cream cheese, try garlic and herb soft cheese for a stronger flavour.

Picnic Lunch

Roasted Chicken Legs

Ingredients:

1 tbsp honey
1 tbsp vinegar
4 tbsp oil
1 tsp paprika
1 tbsp soy sauce
1 tsp sambal oelek
salt and pepper
12 chicken drumsticks

To garnish:
basil

Method:

1 Heat the oven to 180°C (160° fan/350°F/gas 4).

2 Mix together all the ingredients except the chicken drumsticks.

3 Brush the drumsticks generously with the mixture and place in a baking tin or dish. Cook for 15 minutes, then turn over, brush again with the mixture and cook for a further 15 minutes, until the chicken is cooked. To test that the chicken is cooked, insert a skewer into the thickest part of the thigh and check to see if the juices run clear and there is no pink meat.

4 Serve garnished with basil.

Sambal oelek is a red chilli paste. If you prefer a milder flavour, use tomato paste (tomato purée) instead.

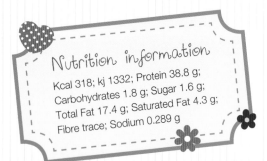

Nutrition information
Kcal 318; kj 1332; Protein 38.8 g;
Carbohydrates 1.8 g; Sugar 1.6 g;
Total Fat 17.4 g; Saturated Fat 4.3 g;
Fibre trace; Sodium 0.289 g

Picnic Lunch

Veggie Burger Sandwiches

Ingredients:

100 g | 3½ oz slightly stale bread, cubed
2 eggs
salt and pepper
grated nutmeg
paprika
100 g | 3½ oz | ½ cup cottage cheese
½ red capsicum (bell pepper), very finely diced
1 can kernel corn (corn kernels or sweet corn), drained
1 small zucchini (courgette), diced
3 tbsp chopped chives
2–4 tbsp breadcrumbs
oil for frying

To serve:
1 large French loaf or baguette
8 lettuce leaves
1–2 tomatoes, sliced
tomato sauce (ketchup)

Method:

1 Put the bread cubes into a bowl. Whisk the eggs with salt, pepper, nutmeg and paprika and pour over the bread. Leave to stand for 10–15 minutes.

2 Add the cottage cheese, vegetables and chives to the bread mixture and mix well. If the mixture is too soft to shape, gradually add the breadcrumbs. Mix well and leave to stand for 5 minutes.

3 Shape the mixture into 8 small burgers.

4 Heat the oil in a frying pan (skillet), to a depth of about 2.5 cm (1 in). Cook the burgers for a few minutes on each side until golden brown. Drain on absorbent kitchen paper.

5 Slice the baguette into 4 pieces. Place 2 burgers in each piece and add the lettuce and tomatoes. Serve with a small bowl of tomato sauce (ketchup).

Nutrition information

Kcal 523; kj 2213; Protein 23.7 g;
Carbohydrates 88.7 g; Sugar 11.9 g;
Total Fat 10.6 g; Saturated Fat 2.4 g;
Fibre 9 g; Sodium 2.124 g

You can replace the cheese with finely chopped firm tofu.

Avocado Dip with Vegetable Sticks

Ingredients:

4 carrots, ends trimmed
4 sticks celery, ends trimmed
1 large ripe avocado
150 mL | 5 fl oz | ⅔ cup soured cream
1 tbsp lime juice

To garnish:
1 cherry tomato, halved

Method:

1 Cut the carrots in half lengthways, then cut them into equal-sized sticks.

2 Cut the celery into equal-sized sticks. Put the vegetables into little serving dishes.

3 Peel away the avocado skin and remove the stone. Roughly chop the flesh and put into a food processor or blender with the soured cream and lime juice. Blend together until smooth.

4 Spoon the avocado dip into small dish and garnish with the cherry tomato halves.

Nutrition information
Kcal 235; kj 971; Protein 3.3 g;
Carbohydrates 18.4 g; Sugar 16.8 g;
Total Fat 16.9 g; Saturated Fat 6.7 g;
Fibre 8.9 g; Sodium 0.086 g

Replace the lime juice with lemon juice for a different flavour.

If not eating the dip immediately, cover and chill until ready to serve.

Picnic Lunch

Lamb Burgers and Aioli

Ingredients:

For the lamb burgers:
500 g | 18 oz minced (ground) lamb
1 clove garlic, crushed
1 small onion, finely chopped
¼ tsp ground turmeric
1 tsp ground coriander
¼ tsp ground cumin
salt and freshly ground black pepper
oil, for brushing

For the aioli:
3 cloves garlic, crushed
2 egg yolks
1 tbsp Dijon mustard
300 mL | 11 fl oz | 1⅓ cups olive oil
½–1 tsp lemon juice
salt and pepper

To serve:
flat bread or pita bread
watercress
sliced tomatoes

Method:

1 Place the minced (ground) lamb in a mixing bowl and add the garlic, onion, turmeric, coriander and cumin. Season well with salt and pepper and mix by hand until combined.

2 Shape the mixture into 4 burgers. Place the burgers on a tray and chill for at least 30 minutes.

3 Heat the grill (broiler).

4 Brush the burgers with a little oil and grill (broil) for about 5–6 minutes each side, until cooked through.

5 For the aioli: put the garlic, egg yolks and mustard into a food processor or blender. Blend into a paste and very slowly drizzle in the olive oil to make a thick mayonnaise-like sauce.

6 Add the lemon juice and season to taste with salt and pepper. Spoon into a serving bowl.

7 Slice open the bread and place the burgers inside with watercress and tomatoes. Serve with the aioli.

Nutrition information
Kcal 1205; kj 4999; Protein 34.3 g;
Carbohydrates 44.5 g; Sugar 4.3 g;
Total Fat 100.3 g; Saturated Fat 20.3 g;
Fibre 2.7 g; Sodium 0.665 g

Don't use extra-lean mince as the fat is needed to help bind the burgers and keep them juicy.

The aioli will keep covered in the refrigerator for up to 2 days.

Tuna Salad Rolls

Ingredients:

4 tbsp mayonnaise
1 tbsp tomato paste (tomato purée)
6–8 tortillas, 18 cm | 7 in diameter
370 g | 13 oz canned tuna, drained
2 large tomatoes, diced
1 red onion, finely sliced
½ iceberg lettuce, shredded
salt and pepper

Method:

1 Mix the mayonnaise with the tomato paste (tomato purée) and spread over the tortillas.

2 Flake the tuna in a bowl and mix with the vegetables. Season to taste with salt and pepper.

3 Divide between the tortillas, roll up and serve.

Nutrition information
Kcal 629; kj 2639; Protein 31.1 g;
Carbohydrates 69.3 g; Sugar 9.3 g;
Total Fat 27.1 g; Saturated Fat 4.2 g;
Fibre 6.1 g; Sodium 0.748 g

You can add other ingredients such as diced cucumber, watercress and torn basil leaves.

117

Strawberry and Soft Cheese Sandwich

Ingredients:

8 slices lightly toasted bread
100 g | 3½ oz | ½ cup cream cheese
4 tsp honey
4 large strawberries, thinly sliced

Method:

1 Roll the toasted bread slices flat with a rolling pin.

2 Using a cookie cutter or card template, cut out a heart from each slice. Using a smaller cutter, cut out the centres of 4 hearts.

3 Spread the heart-shaped slices (without the cutouts) with cheese and drizzle with honey.

4 Arrange the strawberries on the cheese and honey and place the remaining slices of toast on top, pressing down lightly.

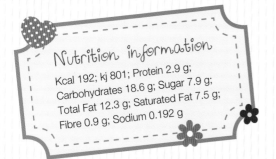

Nutrition information

Kcal 192; kj 801; Protein 2.9 g;
Carbohydrates 18.6 g; Sugar 7.9 g;
Total Fat 12.3 g; Saturated Fat 7.5 g;
Fibre 0.9 g; Sodium 0.192 g

Use a soft mild cream cheese and mild-flavoured honey (e.g. acacia) for the best results.

Picnic Lunch

Cherry, Chocolate and Coconut Squares

Ingredients:

For the base:

200 g | 7 oz | 3 cups desiccated (fine) coconut
400 g | 14 oz | 2 cups white (granulated) sugar
400 g | 14 oz | 2 cups butter
8 eggs
400 g | 14 oz | 3¾ cups plain (all-purpose) flour
3 tsp baking powder
20 mL | ¾ fl oz | 4 tsp coconut syrup
½ tsp almond extract
milk

For the icing (frosting):

300 g | 11 oz milk chocolate, 45% cocoa solids
75 g | 2½ oz | ⅓ cup butter
100 g | 3½ oz | ½ cup glacé (candied) cherries and strawberries, chopped

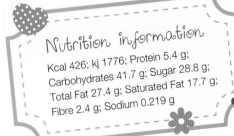

Nutrition information

Kcal 426; kj 1776; Protein 5.4 g;
Carbohydrates 41.7 g; Sugar 28.8 g;
Total Fat 27.4 g; Saturated Fat 17.7 g;
Fibre 2.4 g; Sodium 0.219 g

Method:

1 Heat the oven to 180°C (160° fan/350°F/gas 4). Line a rectangular baking tin with non-stick baking paper.

2 Toast the coconut until golden in a dry frying pan (skillet). Sprinkle with 4–6 tablespoons sugar and stir over the heat until the coconut is lightly caramelised. Set aside and leave to cool.

3 Beat the butter and remaining sugar in a mixing bowl until light and fluffy. Beat in the eggs until smooth.

4 Finely grind the caramelised coconut in a food mill or food processor.

5 Sift the flour and baking powder into the egg mixture. Stir in the coconut. Gradually add the coconut syrup and almond extract. If the mixture is too stiff add milk, a tablespoonful at a time.

6 Spread the mixture in the baking tin and bake for 60–70 minutes until firm.

7 Place the cake on a wire rack and remove the paper. Leave to cool.

8 For the icing (frosting): put the chocolate and butter into a heatproof bowl and melt over a pan of simmering (not boiling) water.

9 Spread the icing over the cake and scatter with the glacé (candied) fruit. When the chocolate is almost set, cut the cake into squares and leave to cool completely.

You could also use plain (dark) or white chocolate, instead of milk chocolate, for the icing.

Toasting the coconut enhances the flavour.

Picnic Lunch

Chocolate Brownies

Ingredients:

350 g | 12 oz plain (dark) chocolate, 70% cocoa solids

250 g | 9 oz | 1⅛ cups butter

3 large eggs

250 g | 9 oz | 1⅛ cups dark brown sugar

55 g | 2 oz | ½ cup plain (all-purpose) flour

1 tsp baking powder

150 g | 5 oz | 1 cup roughly chopped macadamia nuts

Method:

1 Heat the oven to 160°C (140° fan/325°F/gas 3). Grease an 18 x 28 cm (7 x 11 in) baking tin and line the base with non-stick baking paper.

2 Place the chocolate and butter in a pan and heat gently, stirring until melted. Allow to cool slightly.

3 Whisk the eggs in a mixing bowl until pale and frothy, then add the sugar, a spoonful at a time, whisking until thick and glossy.

4 Gently fold in the melted chocolate mixture, until blended.

5 Sift in the flour and baking powder and fold into the mixture with the nuts.

6 Spoon into the tin, level with the back of a spoon and bake for about 40 minutes, until the top has a cracked appearance and the centre is still a little soft to the touch. Cool in the tin for 15 minutes, then place on a wire rack to cool completely. Cut into squares to serve.

Nutrition information

Kcal 408; kj 1701; Protein 3.9 g; Carbohydrates 35.1 g; Sugar 32 g; Total Fat 29.3 g; Saturated Fat 14.1 g; Fibre 1.6 g; Sodium 0.113 g

Do not over-bake or you will lose the famous sticky brownie texture.

You can vary the flavour by using chopped pecan nuts, walnuts or almonds instead of macadamia nuts.

123

Apple and Cranberry Muffins

Ingredients:

250 g | 9 oz | 2¼ cups plain (all-purpose) flour
2½ tsp baking powder
½ tsp bicarbonate of soda (baking soda)
2 tsp ground cinnamon
200 g | 7 oz | 2 cups grated apples, mixed with 1 tbsp lemon juice
100 g | 3½ oz | 1 cup cranberries
1 egg
140 g | 5 oz | ¾ cup white (granulated) sugar
80 mL | 3 fl oz | ⅓ cup sunflower oil
1 tsp vanilla extract
250 mL | 9 fl oz | 1 cup buttermilk
icing (confectioner's) sugar

Method:

1 Heat the oven to 180°C (160° fan/350°F/gas 4). Place paper cases in a 12-hole muffin tin.

2 Mix the flour, baking powder, bicarbonate of soda (baking soda), cinnamon, apples and cranberries in a mixing bowl.

3 Whisk together the egg, sugar, oil, vanilla and buttermilk and mix well.

4 Stir the wet mixture into the dry ingredients and stir until just combined.

5 Spoon the mixture into the paper cases and bake for 25–30 minutes until golden. Cool in the tins for 5 minutes, then place on a wire rack to cool completely.

6 Sift over a little icing (confectioner's) sugar just before serving.

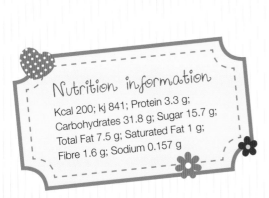

Nutrition information

Kcal 200; kj 841; Protein 3.3 g;
Carbohydrates 31.8 g; Sugar 15.7 g;
Total Fat 7.5 g; Saturated Fat 1 g;
Fibre 1.6 g; Sodium 0.157 g

Different flavours are easy! Just use blueberries, walnuts, chocolate chips or raisins instead of cranberries.

Don't over-mix the dry and wet ingredients; stir until just combined and still lumpy to ensure the muffins are light.

Picnic Lunch

Weights and Measures

Weights and measures differ from country to country, but with these handy conversion charts cooking has never been easier!

Cup Measurements

One cup of these commonly used ingredients is equal to the following weights.

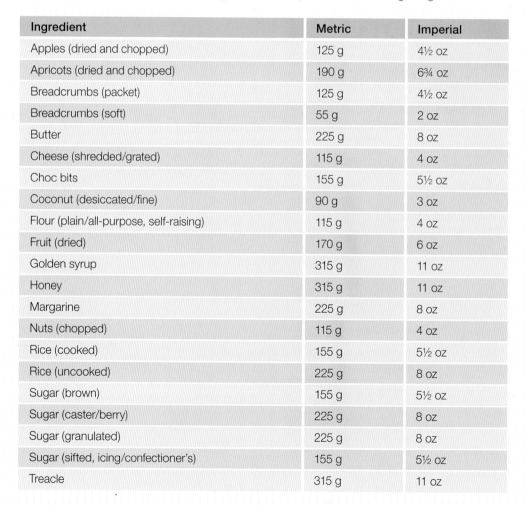

Ingredient	Metric	Imperial
Apples (dried and chopped)	125 g	4½ oz
Apricots (dried and chopped)	190 g	6¾ oz
Breadcrumbs (packet)	125 g	4½ oz
Breadcrumbs (soft)	55 g	2 oz
Butter	225 g	8 oz
Cheese (shredded/grated)	115 g	4 oz
Choc bits	155 g	5½ oz
Coconut (desiccated/fine)	90 g	3 oz
Flour (plain/all-purpose, self-raising)	115 g	4 oz
Fruit (dried)	170 g	6 oz
Golden syrup	315 g	11 oz
Honey	315 g	11 oz
Margarine	225 g	8 oz
Nuts (chopped)	115 g	4 oz
Rice (cooked)	155 g	5½ oz
Rice (uncooked)	225 g	8 oz
Sugar (brown)	155 g	5½ oz
Sugar (caster/berry)	225 g	8 oz
Sugar (granulated)	225 g	8 oz
Sugar (sifted, icing/confectioner's)	155 g	5½ oz
Treacle	315 g	11 oz

Oven Temperatures

Celsius	Fahrenheit	Gas mark
120	250	1
150	300	2
160	320	3
180	350	4
190	375	5
200	400	6
220	430	7
230	450	8
250	480	9

Liquid Measures

Cup	Metric	Imperial
¼ cup	63 mL	2¼ fl oz
½ cup	125 mL	4½ fl oz
¾ cup	188 mL	6⅔ fl oz
1 cup	250 mL	8¾ fl oz
1¾ cup	438 mL	15½ fl oz
2 cups	500 mL	17½ fl oz
4 cups	1 litre	35 fl oz

Spoon	Metric	Imperial
¼ teaspoon	1.25 mL	$\frac{1}{25}$ fl oz
½ teaspoon	2.5 mL	$\frac{1}{12}$ fl oz
1 teaspoon	5 mL	$\frac{1}{6}$ fl oz
1 tablespoon	15 mL	½ fl oz

Weight Measures

Metric	Imperial
10 g	¼ oz
15 g	½ oz
20 g	⅓ oz
30 g	1 oz
60 g	2 oz
115 g	4 oz (¼ lb)
125 g	4½ oz
145 g	5 oz
170 g	6 oz
185 g	6½ oz
200 g	7 oz
225 g	8 oz (½ lb)
300 g	10½ oz
330 g	11½ oz
370 g	13 oz
400 g	14 oz
425 g	15 oz
455 g	16 oz (1 lb)
500 g	17½ oz (1 lb 1½ oz)
600 g	21 oz (1 lb 5 oz)
650 g	23 oz (1 lb 7 oz)
750 g	26½ oz (1 lb 10½ oz)
1000 g (1 kg)	35 oz (2 lb 3 oz)

Weights & Measures

Index

Apple and Cranberry Muffins 124
Avocado Dip with Vegetable Sticks 112
Baked Potato Wedges with Dip 76
Banana Smoothie 104
Bean and Rice Burritos 14
Beef Skewers with Peanut Sauce 12
Berry Breakfast Smoothie 102
Berry Crostata 56
Berry Domes 80
Blueberry Pancakes 96
Boiled Egg and Soldiers 100
Butterfly Buns 48
Cherry, Chocolate and Coconut Squares 120
Chicken and Vegetable Skewers with Rice 18
Chicken Nuggets 70
Chocolate and Butter Cream Cupcakes 64
Chocolate Brownies 122
Chocolate Fondue 28
Chocolate Mousse with Raspberry Sauce 36
Chocolate Pistachio Cookies 44
Chocolate Whoopie Pies 40
Chocolate-Dipped Marshmallows 90
Double-Choc Cupcakes 60
Falafel 72
Fish Finger Dinner 24
French Toast 98
Grilled Fruit Skewers 38
Herbed Chicken Fillets 74
Homemade Lemonade 84
Homemade Popcorn 88
Hot Chocolate with Marshmallows 94

Lamb Burgers and Aioli 114
Layered Cake with Raspberries and Cream 34
Love-Heart Cookies 58
Macaroni and Cheese 20
Marshmallow Choc-Chip Cookies 46
Melon Ball Skewers 82
Nachos with Salsa and Guacamole 78
Pasta and Vegetable Bake 16
Pink Coconut Squares 50
Pizza Muffins 68
Pizza with Ham, Corn and Mushrooms 22
Quesadillas 10
Raspberry Butter Cookies 54
Raspberry Coconut Cake 62
Raspberry Meringues 30
Raspberry Yoghurt Ice-Cream 42
Roasted Chicken Legs 108
Shortbread S'mores 86
Sliders 66
Spaghetti Bolognaise 8
Strawberry and Chocolate Ice-Cream Sandwiches 32
Strawberry and Soft Cheese Sandwich 118
Summer Berry Pudding 26
Sweet and Salty Nuts 92
Tomato Soup with Croutons 6
Tuna Salad Rolls 116
Vanilla Cupcakes 52
Vegetable Wraps 106
Veggie Burger Sandwiches 110